Shirley Patricia Penn
(née Crompton) 1932-2021

MEDITATIONS & POEMS

Shirley Penn

The following items were found in Shirley's personal note book first opened, read, and typed up by her husband, Christopher, after she had died.

CONTENTS

The Incarnation	7
New life	10
Blue beyond blue	11
The garden wall	12
In gratitude	14
Airport antics	15
Dragonfly day	16
Stay and see	18
Hands around the abbey	20
Time ...	21
Faith with fireworks	22
Give a dog a name	24
Alien website	26
We'll fight them in the fields	28
A Glenfall gloria	29
Stable hands	31
Kingfisher afternoon	32
Squirrelling around at Abbey House	34
Marriage - a meditation	35
If only I had learned how to sing!	36
A shopper's saga	40
Hats	43
Indulgences	47

Copyright © 2022 Shirley Penn

The moral right of the author has been asserted.

Apart from any fair dealing for the purposes of research or private study, or criticism or review, as permitted under the Copyright, Designs and Patents Act 1988, this publication may only be reproduced, stored or transmitted, in any form or by any means, with the prior permission in writing of the publishers, or in the case of reprographic reproduction, in accordance with the terms of licences issued by the Copyright Licensing Agency. Enquires concerning reproduction outside those terms should be sent to the publishers.

The Listening People
15 Cleeve Grove
Keynsham,
Bristol, BS31 2HF

ISBN 978-1-915288-02-8

British Library Cataloguing in Publication Data.
A catalogue record for this book is available from the British Library.

Preface

Perhaps it is typical of Shirley's modesty that most of these poems and meditations had not seen the light of day until they were found after her death.

Shirley would sometimes speak at various Mothers' Union events or Church Socials and her gifts of poetry and humour were seen on those occasions. In this collection we can see and hear her gentle faith and her acute awareness of God's creation in all its forms.

Shirley has managed to observe beauty among old and decaying objects, to move from being unable to comprehend the huge problems of the world to appreciating the extreme beauty of the small and delicate creatures around her.

She delights in seeing her first kingfisher and watching the antics of a squirrel. She transforms the eerie observation of an alien website into relief and pleasure at the intricacies of millions of spider webs .

It's not all serious, though. Supermarkets, hats, dog's names and the gift of chocolate have all been written about with Shirley's humour.

These poems we can read and enjoy quickly but the meditations are to be read slowly and allowed to permeate our senses in order to share her faith in God.

The contents of this collection were written, "grounded in faith, trust and love."

Thank you Shirley, my friend,

Revd. Linda Sullivan

THE INCARNATION

I watched as the tiny raindrop crash-landed into the puddle. It fell with a plop! Immediately, miniature concentric waves followed each other to the edge of that muddy pool. I looked again to the centre but the raindrop was nowhere to be seen — it had fragmented on impact. Yet, that very act of breaking enabled the ripples to carry their message of replenishment across the surface and to stir the mud below. My raindrop had gone but it lived on in the water and now others came to join it, swelling the puddle till it reached my feet, then including me in it. I looked at my wellies and marvelled at its cleaning power despite the silt thrown up.

As I stood there revelling, I looked up at the rain cloud above and thought how God's heart must have overflowed with love to give us his most precious gift of his son; of how we longed to receive him as the puddle longed for the raindrop; of how we broke that gift on a cross and yet, in so doing, made it possible for all to share that love...

When God's love laps our hearts we can do nothing more than respond with joy for we know it is this alone can stir the mud and cleanse us...

A WINDOW into PRAYER
(2010)

I want to see Jesus.
Instead, a grimy window pane reflects back the light
Staying my eye on the nearness of the everyday.

How can I see Jesus?
I strain to penetrate the hurting brightness
But my mind is focused on the debris of my carelessness and the litter of my thoughts and deeds
Strewn among the weeds of gossip, greed and doubt.

I need to see Jesus
How far then must I search?
Surely this fence is not of my erecting?
It's far too high and wide.
I had to keep my distance from you Lord
For fear you might ask too much of me.
I sit
And, slowly, circlets of unsatisfied longing draw my eyes
Through the chains which bound me in their prison clasp.
Surely, I'll see Jesus!

For a moment I saw his outstretched arms waiting to embrace me
But 'twas only the gnarled and stunted limbs of a struggling tree
In single combat against a polluted atmosphere
To produce its Springtime newness

And a hope to see Jesus
My gaze led on toward my near horizon —
A brick wall now halts the way
But I must see Jesus.

Determination and desire forced an upward stare
Above, beyond the bricks so assiduously laid to impede
the free range of my mind!
And suddenly within the confines of this small room
I met Jesus

It is surely remarkable to know that Shirley spent the last weeks and days of her life alone in a hospital side ward with a window overlooking a small garden.

NEW LIFE
(2011)

It lay there all winter, broken backed, desolate victim
of the howling autumn gale.
Life roots torn exposed and naked
A gaping chasm where once the embryonic seed in
tiny crack had fallen
To be nurtured to a mighty beech.
I passed it daily
With scarce a glance after that initial shocking sight;
Until this morning, as the warming sun of early Spring
Shafting through these trees more fortunately
standing
Lighted on my tree, leafless cold - But no, not dead
For from a crevice new life transformed that lifeless
trunk.
Strong green shoots—not beechen,
How could they be?
And from the spreading circlet of vibrant tender leaves

On slender stem of paler green
A glorious golden crown
Fashioned from a myriad sun-drop petals
The humble, kingly, dandelion.

BLUE beyond BLUE
(2013)

Today I looked up at Heaven
Penetrating the blue beyond blue
To God.
Half-formed puffs of cloud like distracting thoughts
Skimmed across the ethereal blueness of my mind
Disintegrating into wisps, absorbed in the subconscious;
Swiftly pursued by others, willing my inward eyes
To focus on the near and disregard
The blue beyond
Until, from the periphery of my vision,
The bird, gently circling
Majestic, silently scornful
Of those inconsequential clouds beneath,
Undeviating, soaring, in a solitary freedom
Drew my heart in Godward spiral
To the blue beyond blue
To heaven.

Inspired by a circling Buzzard watched on a country walk, an allegory of the Holy Spirit.

THE GARDEN WALL
(2013)

Alone, in the stillness of a winter garden
I mused in silence on the dry-stone wall,
Wondering idly what creative hands had fashioned
Not a barrier 'tween patio and garden bed
But a seam of harmonious strength.
Drawing my gaze along its lichened length.
What deep discovering eye had searched among the irregular stones?
What work-worn fingers had shaped and smoothed
To lay the one upon the other?
This rough-edged rock, unpromising lies now
Improbable, unmoving 'gainst that flat
unlikely limestone slice.
Sustaining and sustained
With nought but air to hold them in their own allotted space.
Yet to produce
Such bond of usefulness so pleasing in its symmetry
This wall must be firmly planted in the garden earth.
My thoughts ran on
Are we, too,
Like stones chosen by our Creator placed with care?
Some rough and angular, abrasive, cold.
Others worn to smoothness by the chances of life?
Each called upon to fulfil a dual role
Supported and supportive

And surrounding all, invisible, essential,
The Holy Spirit fills the spaces of our disharmony
And binds us all in unity
Grounded in faith and trust and love
We may stand with confidence
Built by God into a world of harmony.

IN GRATITUDE
(1970)

I lay there Lord, my life ebbing out;
The nurses passing, pausing, passing on.
I closed my eyes to shut out pain and fear
But that just locked them in the more secure
And made my grip on starchy sheets the more intense.

Suddenly—
A voice above my head
Not a whisper as to the dying
But a confident assurance
Willing me relax, open my eyes
And see
A man, large in every sense, leaned down
Hands reaching out
Broad hands, gentle in their soft caress.
I saw; I heard;
"We'll do our best to save you both, but we'll concentrate on mother."
I thank you, Lord, for that voice, those hands
Restoring life.
I give it back to you each day
In grateful love.

Back in 1960 Shirley was grievously ill in hospital, with acute pancreatitis near her second full term pregnancy. Our son was born but died within twenty-four hours. Her surgeon was Mr H Trapnell.

AIRPORT ANTICS

Ten big aeroplanes standing in a line,
One took off too soon, then there were nine.

Nine big aeroplanes up at Lulsgate,
One went to Edinburgh and then there were eight.

Eight big aeroplanes, flying off to Devon,
One got lost en route, then there were seven.

Seven big aeroplanes, need an engine fix,
One couldn't be repaired, then there were six.

Six big aeroplanes, about to arrive,
One took off again, then there were five.

Five big aeroplanes, with engines set to roar,
One failed to make a noise, then there were four.

Four big aeroplanes, flying out to sea,
One turned inland, then there were three.

Three big aeroplanes, waiting for their crew,
One pilot lost his way, then there were two.

Two big aeroplanes thought they'd have come fun,
One couldn't hold his fuel, then there was one.

One big aeroplane feeling all alone,
He took off for Spain, then there were none.

DRAGONFLY DAY
(2018)

I sat alone on the late summer hillside
Pondering the smoothed down emerald quilt below
Square-stitched by darker threads of hedgerow
And sparkled silver line drawn ruler-straight across the vale.

Aloft, a lazy cloud hung painted
On a cobalt canvas.
Nothing to disturb that tranquil scene,
But then... a far-off drone assailed my half tuned ear.

Louder now until, within my upward gaze
An insect hovered, giant, large
Utilitarian, man-made
Growing ever larger, till it filled my cloud
Turning it to dark from white.
Man, machine and mission in one determination,
Buzzed relentlessly through
the silence of that sun warmed day.

Compelling me to hear, and watch,
While this creation of man's desire for flight,
With no sense of urgency displayed,
retreated from my eyes and ears
To become a tiny speck where earth met sky,

Then gone.

My thoughts retracted to a closer view,
I watched with wonder as yet another craft
Poised quivering in the gentle air,
Hovered with consummate ease,
Then softly dropped to settle at my feet.

No raucous buzz, no turning blade;
instead, translucent, fluttering, silent wings,
Delicate, perfect as only God could fashion,
The dragonfly cast its magic spell
To hold me enchanted, breath-held,
Each motionless in the moment
Until it, too, determined in its mission
Flew lightly past
To reach another patch of sunlit heaven.

STAY and SEE
(2017)

Not much here, I'll pass on by—
But
Something urges me down that path
Between two rows of shady trees to a
Sunlit circle of new-mown grass
A vast old tree trunk centred there
Branches hewn and lying all around—
Forlorn, forgotten.
No life, no hope – no need for me to stay,
Yet somehow compelled, I sit on a flattened stump.
The autumn sun casting shadows
On the grey-brown carpet
Of bark and twigs beneath my feet
Not much here. I'd best move on—
But
What's that peeping through the bark,
Barely visible to my unsensed eye?
A tiny toadstool. All alone?
No, no, there's more and more and even some
In cluster large around a log;
Creating life where I thought was none,
Creating hope, willing me to stay and see
That here amongst the bark-strewn earth
Are tiny plants of vivid green,
Nodding and waving in the cooling breeze.

A moment longer before I take my leave—
A myriad insects dancing to the sun and
Suddenly—
With shimmering translucent, rainbow wings,
A damsel fly alights upon my shoe.
Oh, now I cannot move
Until—
As sudden she darts across the grass to find her mate
And I am left to wonder that the hand
Which fashioned all these tiny things
With such incomparable precision
Should then, with larger vision, sculpt
That gnarled and twisted trunk
And, what's more, should think of me.

HANDS around the ABBEY

Tiny squirrel hands, clasping hazel nuts so daintily:
Green fingered gardeners hands, promoting growth and light:
Inquisitive visitors' hands compelled to touch and feel and point:
Unseen, sculpting hands, that shaped and built a house,
More lofty than the tallest tree—
seeking to confine their God within its walls:
Dark, jealous hands of power that wrought
Destruction, tears and sorrow,
Yet released that self-same God into the freedom of his world.
And now, more recently, the careful hands of visionaries
Restoring beauty from the chaos, reclaiming history
For all to see.
I stayed a while, my own hands still,
For what had they to offer in this holy place?
Till suddenly a buzzard circled overhead—
A messenger with silent cry
So loud and clear
Reach up, bend down, touch flower and leaf and tree
To grasp the bounteous hand of God within your own,
Then go and hold another's hand and share
His gracious gifts of love.

TIME...

Time is of the essence;
Commodity of contrasts;
Desired by most,
Dreaded by some.
We all need time but where do we look for it?
Can we find it?
Some clever people manage to make time.
How?
With what?
And at what cost?
Others take time
From where?
Do they steal it from those who say they have none to spare?
Can time be bought?
From whom?
And then there's borrowed time -
Who would lend so precious a possession?
Knowing it can never be repaid?
What of those who have too much?
And cannot find a way to use it?
Isn't it strange and paradoxical
That in this clock watching world the folk
Who make, take, and find time
Are the self-same ones who straight way give, share and spend it!

FAITH with FIREWORKS

1.

A bush fire on the mountain
And a voice that made Moses say, "Oh
Yes, Lord I'll give Pharaoh your order
Your people he has to let go!"

2.

God saw Gideon's large army
And said, "No it has to be small
Your swords and torches flaming
Will make the Midianites fall."

3.

Mary was a red hot cracker
Attested by all of the men
But Jesus soon ended her antics
By saying "Don'ft do it again!"

4

Zacchaeus went up like a rocket
And hid in a very tall tree
But came to earth at Jesus' calling
"Zacchaeus, I'm coming to tea."

5

Martha was tied to her housework
Like a wheel that's pinned to a tree

Sending out sparks of annoyance
'till Jesus' soft words set her free.

6

Mary, her sister, was different.
No squib or jumping jack she
But gently glowing for Jesus
She quietly stayed at his knee.

7

A Centurion of Rome at the Cross
Stood watching in horror and shame.
Then a candle inside him ignited
And his life was never the same.

8

The Disciples heard a loud whooshing
And looked up to see a bright flame.
Know then that God's Spirit was with them
So went out fired up in his name.

9

We all have a faith deep inside us
Let Jesus' love set it alight
Then, as his flame kindles within you
Go out and spread your delight.

GIVE a DOG a NAME

Our first dog was a pup called *Pixie*
A pretty black Labrador cross,
But he grew 'till his name sounded silly
Though I don't think He gave it a toss.

Next came a little King Charles mix up
One look at him was enough
To make us exclaim simultaneously
"Oh, You're re a right little S*cruff!"*

He needed a friend to keep him at home,
So we found one who too, had a need
A mongrel we decided to call *Tansy*
'Cos she was yellow and rather a weed.

Toffee was seven when we had her
Though Dinkie her original name
But tiny she wasn't, nor dinkie
Just red-coated, so Toffee she quickly became.

There was one which we found by the wayside
So thin we thought it her end
We then hastily christened her *Twiggy*
And she lived and thrived many years with a friend.

The next to join us was a retriever.
Again a name choice we must make
But as sci-fi fans it was easy
Being dog number seven he was *Blake*.

When we needed another we found *Honey*
Who seemed gentle and loving and sweet.
But her mission in life we discovered
Was to kill every dog we might meet!

And now we have little *Millie*
A Jack Russell or should it be Jill?
At 13 she's no longer as lively
But still all our days she can fill.

So if an a name for a pet you're searching
Here's a thought you may like to consider.
As long as there's love, walkies and food,
Whatever you call them won't matter!

Our family were great dog lovers and thoroughly enjoyed the dogs we were privileged to keep through many years. This little poem names and remembers them all.

ALIEN WEBSITE
(Lambert's Castle Heath, Dorset)

An early Autumn afternoon;
Warm sun, breaking through dark clouds
Dispelling the recent storm
Transformed the gorse-thick common to an alien land,
Enmeshed in gossamer threads of glistening silver,
Seemingly unbroken and unbreakable,
Stretching across the once green hillside to the edge of sight.

I stood transfixed in awe and apprehension.
Had unseen invaders from a far flung galaxy Imprisoned
the newly purpled heather and blackberry-laden bramble
for some sinister intent, impossible to contemplate?
And, if daring my step to stray from the well-worn grassy path,
Might I too be wrapped and bound and held?

With silent stealth I edged towards the nearest bush,
Tentative, Unsure, Fearing what may lurk
within that dark forbidding mass
Of twisted briar and tangled bracken.
And there, with light relief and up-surging joy I then perceived

No unearthly being, or strange creature from another world
Transported here through space and time
to weave its magic on my mind.

But just a humble, earthbound spider
Suspended in its own amazing self-created web
So intricately woven, waiting, resting, certain that
those delicate strands hard-wrought to perfection,
Would ere long hold fast food for today,
and life for tomorrow.

WE'LL FIGHT THEM IN THE FIELDS

1

There he stood, that warrior brave,
No aid for him was near;
Fiercely he struck to right and left
Attempting the foe to scare.

2

The day was hot, the ground was parched,
His war cry rent the air;
Alone he stood with the enemy.
Yet nothing he seemed to fear.

3

All day long he stood his ground,
But there on the grassy plain;
The enemy advanced with stealth:
Forward, and back again.

4

And as the sun began to set
Was heard a resounding crack!
The bull, triumphant now, has slain
The last fly on his back!

A GLENFALL GLORIA

1

Lord for all your colours here,
We praise your precious name;
For silver in the birch and pine,
For gold in pansy, marjoram and sun,
We praise your precious name;
For emerald shades in every tree,
And burnished copper beech,
Wisteria in her amethyst chain,
We praise your precious name.

2

Lord for all the sounds of life,
We praise your own sweet name;
For lilt of lark high up above,
For cheeky robin's chatter,
We praise your own sweet name;
For drone of bees among the flowers,
For trilling brook o'er stones,
And whispered conversations near,
We praise your own sweet name.

3

Lord for all that we can touch,
We praise your caring name;
For silky laurel, prickly thorn,

for mossy flagstones rough,
We praise your caring name;
For metal sculptures smooth and cold,
For wooden seats with welcome arms,
And feathery fronds of fern and fennel,
We praise your caring name.

4

Lord, for all we taste and smell,
We praise your holy name;
For all the scents of blossoms sweet,
      and fragrant tang of herbs,
We praise your holy name;
For everything we see and do,
For life, and love, and joy,
For all creation by your hand,
We praise your holy name.

Glenfall is a Christian retreat house near Cheltenham, Gloscestershire.

STABLE HANDS
(2017)

Mary's hands – relaxed after hours of gripping
the hard wooden board,
the straw,
Joseph,
whatever came near,
now her newly maternal fingers caress
in fear, in joy,
at the wonder of this firstborn life.

Joseph's hands – reliable, gripping the oil-lit lantern,
spreading light, comfort in that dank, dark, cavern:
'till, with strong arms outstretched
gentle, loving,
he laid the babe in the make-shift bed.

Shepherd's hands, gnarled, hard used,
smelling of sheep, wood smoke, hillside,
gripping staves in awe, they kneel, trembling, reaching out,
yet not daring to touch those tiny fingers in the
manger. Did they perceive with dim-lit rheumy eyes
those new born hands, fragile, open,
would cradle with compassion a world as yet
unknown; the fulfilment here of God's promise from
eternity?

KINGFISHER AFTERNOON
(1996)

Dripping trees not yet awakened by Spring's new call;
diamond droplets where soon will cluster emerald buds;
soft mud enveloping each silent step.
No sound save the occasional coo of the pigeon
seeking shelter among barren twigs,
and the busy chatter of the stream gushing over grey stones and old logs,
hustling debris down to join a greater tide.
No stopping – too far to go, too much to do.
No time! No time!

Then suddenly, a slowing in the breakneck speed,
the narrow channel now becomes a wider pool –
absorbing, damming, devoid of movement,
impenetrable, sluggish,
no shimmer of light to lift the heart.
The ivory rods of last year's reeds stand straight,
unreachable, unreached;
a monument to the Autumn death;
A tiny wilderness in that dank and dreary pool.

Until –
a momentary vision amid the tangle of the reedy clump,
a startling flash more brilliant hued than any jewel.

Perceived on the eye of reality?
Or merely the flicker of a dream not yet fulfilled?
Surely it must be there?
I hold my breath, my eyes hard fixed on those unbending reeds
and – yes – it's there again,
this time more real than thoughts which hover on the edge of reason.
This time the reeds have parted to reveal
God's promise in the glory of a bird.
With wings outstretched it darts across the pool,
fusing the air with iridescent blue;
and in its wake, green shoots appear along that sodden path,
bright crimson branches of a marshy bush,
young catkins dancing overhead –
fresh signs of life where none till then I'd seen,
the once unlovely pool now glistens with translucent light.

My heart revives and I rejoice once more,
For there, in the flight of that one small bird,
I glimpsed the love of God shed wide.

SQUIRRELLING AROUND at ABBEY HOUSE
(2013)

Where shall I hide it? Is this a good place?
No, I've rather a big nut and there's not enough space.
How about this spot close by the tree?
Not far to go for my Breakfast or Tea!
But how can I trust all my sisters and brothers?
If it's obvious to me, then it must be for others.
I'll just keep scampering about in this beautiful grass,
Sure, when I find it, the right place I'll not pass.
Now what about here – there's no one around:
Quick, into the hole, and away with a bound;
bobbing and leaping, making notes to remember
where I must dig, come hungry December.
Wheeeeeeeee..........................
Isn't life great, Isn't life good –
God gives me my larder as well as my food!

Abbey house at Glastonbury was the Bath &Wells retreat house for many years.

MARRIAGE – A MEDITATION

Marriage is like a diamond
At first – rough and colourless with little indication of it's hidden potential
But time gradually wears away the roughness,
Revealing many facets, all inter-dependent,
And creating many colours of life:–
Love
Physical sharing
Times good and bad
Companionship
Trust
Care
Respect
Togetherness
Yet allowing each other's "me-time"
Willingness to go the extra mile
Readiness to say, "I'm sorry"
All needing perseverance, honesty, tolerance to shape that diamond – marriage
To become memorable, meaningful,
with Christ the central source of light shining
throughout the days and years...

Shirley Penn

(Married to Christopher for 64 years)

IF *ONLY* I HAD LEARNED HOW TO SING!
(1983)

No, it's all right I'm not the 'Oly ghost
Until now I was one of the 'Eavenly 'Ost
But there's been such a ding-dong
All over a sing song
And now I'm back here as a mortal —
Well almost…

2.

Oh, if only I'd learned how to sing
When I was down here as an earthling
But whenever I tried to
Folks all said, "O must you?
We'd rather you'd do anything but sing!"

3.

As an infant I was sure I could render
My favourite, "Away in a manger"
But in the school I was at
My teacher said, "Flat!"
When I thought was just sweet and tender.

4.

At reciting I was top of the class
And my acting was more than a "Pass"
So I thought I'd no fears
When all was in tears
As I soared through my tonic – sol – fas.

5.
I stood on the stage for my solo
And sang all the notes high and low
But instead of, "Encore!"
They all shouted "No More!"
Until you can reach that top Doh! .

6.
I hadn't a clue what they meant
Told my teacher I thought they'd been sent
She replied "Yes you're right —
We've all had such a fright
I'm going too!" And so saying she went.

7.
Throughout all my childhood and teens
To join choirs I often had dreams
But instead of, "BO"
My friends whispered, "Oh no
Do shut your mouth, if you see what we means (not here please).

8.
I had to be bolder
So I opened my mouth
And all over the south
I found I been given the cold shoulder.

9.
Still I continued to nurse my ambition
That one day I'd give an audition
And my, "Rule Britannia!
Would outdo Tekanawa
And Promenaders would say "Bravo!"
"What a rendition!"

10.
But as the years passed by I could see
That the world and my voice didn't agree
Then one day in the park
St. Peter gave me a harp
And said that Cloud number 5 would be fine.

11.
He then said, "It's Gabriel's fear
The 'eavenly choir's one short this year
And with just three months to go
To the grand Christmas show,
You'd better get practising now, d'you hear?

12.
With my harp I really began training
'Till I thought to myself—Yes, I'm gaining
But as I flew by The clouds started to cry
And folks down here said "Will it ever stop raining?"

13.
Still I kept practising the tune till I knew it
And was sure Gabriel'd say I could do it
But as the Christmas angels sang
And the heavenly trumpets rang
He shouted: "Get out number 5—you just blew it!"

14.
Well it fair made my poor ears to ring
And caused the feathers to droop on my wing
And now all I can do is entertain you
Oh, if only I'd learned how to sing.

I think Shirley had a reasonably good singing voice –Christopher

A SHOPPER'S SAGA

1.

To go shopping was once a great pleasure,
Where help and kind words would abound;
And you sat on a chair and just waited
While the shopkeeper did the running around.
"This cheese comes highly commended,
It's really the best in the store
And the bacon was fresh in this morning,
Shall I cut you just two rashers – or more?"

2.

Then along came the markets they called, 'super'
With large posters to tempt you inside,
And trolleys that just wouldn't go forward
Down aisles that weren't very wide.
So they widened the aisles, put in more shelving,
Making a much bigger and busier store;
Now to do all your shop in one morning
Is like running a marathon, more.

3.

To find what you want is a puzzle.
"Where's the logic?" I often beseech.
And then I eventually spot it
High up on a shelf I can't reach.
With my trolley I head for a checkout;

Which queue is the shortest? I ponder.
Is it this one or that over there?
Uncertain, I bemusedly wander.

4.

I stop where I think I'll be lucky.
Unload all my goods on the belt;
Then immediately find I am worried –
My frozen goods may yet start to melt;
'Cos the lady in front's got her card out
But cannot remember her PIN.
She tapped in four digits quite cheerfully
Only to find they were 'no win'.

5.

The next time I took myself shopping
I could see once again something new;
There were customers standing quite helpless
With scarcely a checkout in view.
"Self serve," I was told, "is the 'In thing'.
With speed as the ultimate plan;
You just have to place every item
On this machine, the bar code to scan."

6.

I held out my very first purchase,
And stood there in trembling and dread,
For the machine now began talking

"Please ask for assistance", it said.
I looked round for someone to help me
But no one seemed very near;
And meanwhile the machine kept repeating,
'Till I said, "O shut up, I can hear!"

7.

At last I got it all sorted,
The machine then asked me to pay;
I offered a note which it swallowed up quick,
"Take your change", I next heard it say.
I picked up the cash to put in my purse,
But that voice wouldn't leave me alone
"Pick up your bags, your shopping's complete."
"Go away," I replied, "I don't like your tone."

8.

Now, shopping on line's all the fashion,
You just need your password and PIN
Plus an alternative list for each item,
'Cos the one that you want's never in.
But this morning I went down the High Street
And found to my greatest delight
The Greengrocer, the Butcher and Baker
Were still happy to serve and polite.

HATS
(1977)

Last week I went to Cribbs Causeway,
Lured by that magic word, 'SALE'.
I went straight to the store that I'm fond of
And visits each time without fail.
It wasn't the crop tops and minis I was after
What? Show me belly?
Like on the telly.
No, give me long trousers or skirt – with a shirt.

2

I did linger a moment in lingerie
'Cos that's always good for a laugh.
And I thought – cor fancy shivering in one of they things
When you climbs out of a steaming hot bath.
The words, 'BIG REDUCTIONS' I don't think referred to the cost
But I do think it's funny
the way folks'll pay money
for a little transparent bit – with a slit.

3

I plunged on to the back of the store
with barely a trace of a glance
at the shoes: and the perfumes failed to attract.
Then I stood there in a trance.

No matter I'd been jostled and bruised and back home
They'd say with a grin
When they see'd me walk in
with me trophy and prize - 'What all that – for a hat?'

4

You see, I've got this thing about hats.
I just love all those feathers and posies
Perched on top of those white plastic models
With their haughty superior noses.
I searched all along and found one I was sure
Was just made for me.
Then I looked round to see
If the assistant was hovering - 'cos that's bothering.

5

It was beautiful straw, this creation
With ribbons and roses all round
But when I tried it on with great hopefulness
I knew it just suited me, down to the ground!
So I reached for another, 'Smart little number,' I thought.
But I put it back quick
'Cos I didn'ft look chic.
In fact much more of an old duck – worse luck.

6

I eagerly picked up another
With the greatest of reverence and care.

Oh, how I wished I'd taken the trouble
To get something done to me hair.
I was convinced this fantastic confection of flowers
In the prettiest of pink
Would make everyone think.
Yes, I've chosen it right — what a beautiful sight.

7

I turned to find the assistant
Feeling really as pleased as could be
When all of a sudden in the mirror
A remarkable picture I see
A very fat lady standing behind me
Had on my green bonnet
With the patches of ginger upon it
Which I'd put on one side — while others I tried

8

I stood there in amazement and wonder
And watched as she turned to the door.
She didn't even offer to pay for the thing
But calmly walked out of the store.
Then I laughed and I laughed till I very near cried
'Cos that was my very old hat
The one that Tiddles my cat
Had used last month as a 'sit- in' for having her kittens!

9

Well, I had to do something about it.
I hadn't a hat to wear home,
So I took a quick look in the mirror
And tidied my locks with a comb.
I spoke to meself most severely.
Now don't be silly and buy something frilly
It's got to be something that's warm – for the farm.

10

But it wasn't the least bit of use
I just couldn't resist buying this,
And then I decided that this one
Was too good a bargain to miss!
Oh I am a fool to meself with me hats.
I came out of the store with four bonnets or more
And not one I could wear – I just wouldn't dare!

11

But me money hasn't been wasted
As you'll see if you come down our way.
I've found a good use for me bonnets
And I looks at them all every day.
You see I've a very small holding back home
And when I walks down me fields
There's Daisy me Cow and Lily me sow
All haughty couture while keeping the flies – out of their eyes!

INDULGENCES

When you open this parcel please don't be grey
And feel you'll simply give it away
'Cos just <u>one</u>, each day
While you work, rest and play,
Is the very best way
For keeping those 'blues' at bay.
So share them together, whatever the weather
And don't give a toss what others may say.
But remember, don't keep this box on display
For Josie to acquire with little delay.
So this gift bears our love,
And sincerely we pray
You'll enjoy all the contents 'till New Year's day
                              (or beyond!).

This rhyme accompanied a tin of Mars miniatures. Josie is the family's pet Labrador.

100% of the proceeds from this book benefit Bath and Wells Diocesan Mothers' Union.

www.ingramcontent.com/pod-product-compliance
Lightning Source LLC
Chambersburg PA
CBHW020303030426
42336CB00010B/892